Vintcent's French Food Dictionary

HARRIMAN HOUSE LTD

43 Chapel Street
Petersfield
Hampshire
GU32 3DY
GREAT BRITAIN

Tel: +44 (0)1730 233870
Fax: +44 (0)1730 233880

email: enquiries@harriman-house.com
website: www.harriman-house.com

First published in Great Britain in 2004

ISBN 1-8975-9748-7

British Library Cataloguing in Publication Data
A CIP catalogue record for this book can be obtained from the
British Library.

Cover painting by Michael Stockdale
View Michael's paintings at www.whiterockgallery.com

Printed and bound by Ashford Colour Press

Acknowledgements

I should like to thank 'Mushroom Man' Phil Dean for explaining the different types of edible fungus that he makes available at Covent Garden, and for being so patient with me. Also, Philip Jenks for being rash enough to publish this little book, and my son James for retrieving all the data that I lost so often on my PC.

This small work is dedicated, as always, to Wendy.

INTRODUCTION

This dictionary of food has been written for all those English-speaking visitors to France who choose to cook for themselves. It is not a book of recipes, nor does it describe any dishes or courses that you will be offered in a restaurant or café.

Many people rent a house, villa or apartment, or stay in a mobile home, caravan or tent, when having a holiday or touring through France, and they enjoy the pleasures of self-catering in a country where so much good food is so plentiful.

Most visitors will use recipes written in English, and many will be bewildered by the variety of different names of the meat, fish and vegetables in the supermarkets, shops and market stalls. French cuts of meat are often dissimilar to those we are used to buying in the UK, and very often the shop assistants or stall holders do not speak English. Anyone who makes an obvious effort to ask for their purchases in the national language will receive much more help from the local people than otherwise.

In some cases, there is more than one name for the same thing, because they are called different names in different regions. For example, the fish that we call 'sea bass' in English is known as 'loup de mer' along the coast of France that borders the Mediterranean, and 'barr' along the Atlantic coast.

Cheeses and wines have been kept to a minimum because there are so many of each available throughout that lovely country that this small guide would become far too big and cumbersome to carry round the shops with you, which would defeat the object of having a small, portable reference aid to food shopping.

Also, there are many reference books on those two items that describe the cheeses and wines in great detail, region by region. The basic essentials needed for cooking are the only ones that have been included.

At the back of the book I have put some helpful tips for use when buying such items as sliced meat or ham when you may want the slices to be thicker or thinner, or, for harder or softer cheese for example. A table of comparative heat settings between gas and electric ovens is shown, along with a guide to pronunciation.

France has a lot to offer, and the people are generally helpful and polite. Regular use of the magic phrases *'s'il vous plaît'* and *'merçi'* will work wonders, and help to cement the *entente cordiale*.

Happy shopping.

Charles Vintcent

July 2004

B

bacon

fat streaky	lard *m*
smoked back	bacon *m*
a rasher of bacon	une tranche *f* de lardon
streaky bacon	lard *m* entrelardé
lean bacon	lard *m* maigre
smoked bacon	lard *m* fumé

beef — bœuf *m*

cut from the small end of fillet of beef	filet *m* mignon see also *lamb/mutton*
fillet steak	filet *m* de bœuf, tournedos *m*
sirloin steak	faux-fillet *m*; bifteck *m* dans l'aloyau
rump steak	rumsteck *m*
slice of rump steak	rumsteck *m* boeuf aiguillette
piece of steak trimmed	piece *f* parée de boeuf à bifteck
rib of beef	côte de bœuf *m*
loin chop	côte première de bœuf *m*
entrecote	entrecôte *f*

stewing steak	bœuf *m* à faire cuire en ragoût
shin of beef	jarret *m* de bœuf
shin of beef with bone	jarret *m* de boeuf avec os
shin of beef without bone	jarret *m* de boeuf sans os
braising steak	bœuf *m* à cuire en daube
frying steak	bœuf *m* à faire frire
brisket of beef	poitrine *f* de bœuf
brisket of beef with bone to roast	poitrine *f* de boeuf avec os à rotir
brisket of beef without bone to boil	poitrine *f* de boeuf sans os à bouiller
silverside	gîte *m* à la noix
topside	tende *f* de tranche de bœuf
neck of beef	collier *m* de bœuf
flank of beef	flanchet *m* de bœuf; bavette *f*
rump or buttock of beef	culotte *f* de boeuf
chuck of beef	paleron *m* de bœuf
shoulder	épaule *f* de bœuf
lean meat from the shoulder	macreuse *f* de boeuf
calf's head	tête *f* de veau
calf's sweetbreads	ris *m* de veau
sirloin	aloyau *m* de boeuf
top of the sirloin	bavette *f* aloyau de boeuf à bifteck
slice (round)	rouelle *f* de boeuf
minced beef	haché *m* de boeuf

lank of beef	hampe *f* de boeuf
wing rib of beef	côte *f* d'aloyau
prime cut	onglet *m*
boar (wild)	sanglier *m*
bone marrow	moelle *f*
brawn	fromage *m* de tête
	fromage *m* de cochon

C

capercailzie	coq *m* de bruyère
capon	chapon *m*
chicken	poulet *m*
recently hatched	poussin *m*
young cockerel	coquelet *m*
free range	poulet *m* fermier
boiling fowl	poule *f*
chicken livers	foies *m* de volaille
chicken liver paté	pâté *m* de fois de volaille
chicken legs	cuisses *f* de volaille
chicken cutlets	côtelettes *f* de volaille
smoked chicken	poulet *m* fumé
breast of chicken	blanc *m* de volaille
wing	aile *f*
smoked chicken	poulet *m* fumé
chicken giblets	abatis *m* de volaille
corn fed chicken	poulet *m* de grain
fattened chicken	poularde *f*

D

duck — canard *m*

thin slice from the breast	aiguillette *f* de canard
carcass	carcasse *f*
gizzard	gésier *m*
plucked	plumé
trussed	préparé pour rôtir
drawn and prepared	vidé et paré
mallard	colvet *m*
teal	sarcelle *f*
widgeon	siffleur *m*
wild duck	canard *m* sauvage
male duck	caneton *m*
female duck	canette *f*
duck paté	mousse *f* de canard
duck liver paté	pâté *m* de fois de canard
smoked duck	canard *m* fumé
duck legs	cuisses *f* de canard
duck breasts	magret *m* de canard
duck's gizzard	gésiers *m* de canard
slice of duck breast	tranche *f* de canard
smoked and dried	fumée et seche
conserve of duck	confit *m* de canard

F

fowl (see also *poultry*)	volaille *f*
frog's legs	cuisses *f* de grenouilles

G

game	gibier *m*
game pie	pâte *m* de gibier
giblets	abats *m*
goat	chèvre *f*
kid	chevreau *m*
goose	oie *f*
goose liver paté	pâté *m* de fois gras
smoked goose	oie *f* fumé
goose legs	cuisses *f* d'oie
goose breasts	blanc *m* d'oie
grouse	grouse *m;* tétras *m*
guinea fowl	pintade *f*
young guinea fowl	pintadeau(x) *m*
gull's eggs	oefs *m* de mouette

H

hare	lièvre *m*
leveret	levraut *m*
saddle of hare	râble *m* de lièvre
ham	jambon *m*
parma ham	jambon *m* de parme

cooked ham	jambon *m* cuit
dry cured ham	jambon *m* de pays
haunch of venison	quartier de chevreuil *m*
horse meat	viande *f* de cheval

K

kid	chevreau *m* (male goat)
	chevrette *f* (she-goat)
kidney	rognon *m*
lamb's kidneys	rognon *m* d'agneau
pig's kidneys	rognon *m* de porc

L

lamb	agneau *m*
suckling lamb	agneau *m* de lait
leg	gigot *m* d'agneau
half leg	gigot *m* d'agneau racourci
lamb shank	jarret *m* d'agneau
shoulder	épaule *f* d'agneau
shoulder half boned	épaule *f* d'agneau désossée
chop	côtelette *f* d'agneau
saddle	selle *f* d'agneau
undercut from saddle	filet *m* mignon
rack	carré *f* d'agneau
best end of neck	collet *m* d'agneau
breast	poitrine *f* d'agneau

undercut	côte *m* filet d'agneau
rib of lamb	côte *m* d'agneau
middle neck cutlets of lamb	côtes *f* découvertes
slice of leg of lamb	tranche *f* gigot d'agneau
with bone/without bone	avec os/sans os
lamb's heart	coeur *m* d'agneau
lamb's liver	foie *m* d'agneau
lamb's sweetbreads	ris *m* d'agneau
marrow bone	os *m* à moelle
mutton	mouton *m*
saddle of mutton	selle *f* de mouton
undercut from saddle	filet *m* mignon
scrag of mutton	collet *m* de mouton
sheep's head	tête *f* de mouton
sheep's trotters	pieds *m* de mouton
lean meat	maigre
lean pork	maigre de porc
lights	mou *m*
liver	fois *m* (pl. *foies*)
calf's liver	fois *m* de veau
lamb's liver	fois *m* d'agneau
pig's liver	foie *m* de cochon

M

minced meat	viande *f* hachée
minced beef	haché de bœuf *m*
minced lamb	haché d'agneau *m*

O

offal - beef, pork — abats *m*
ortolan — ortolan *m*
ox tongue — langue *f* de boeuf

P

partridge — perdrix *f* (pl. perdreau)
pâté - (pork, duck, goose, chicken, game etc.) — pâté *m*
paté with mushrooms — pâté *m* forestière
pheasant - cock — faisan *m*
pheasant - hen — faisane *f*
pigeon — pigeon *m*
    wood pigeon — pigeon *m* ramier
    young pigeon, squab — pigeonneau *m*
pig — cochon
    pig's trotters — pieds *m* de cochon (porc)
    pig's trotters uncooked — pieds *m* de cochon (porc) cru
    pig's liver — foie *m* de cochon (porc)
    pig's head — tête *f* de cochon
    suckling pig — cochon *m* de lait; porcelet *m*
plover — vanneau *m;* pluvier *m*
    plover's eggs — Œufs *m* de vanneau
pork — porc *m*
    leg — jambon *m*
    shoulder — épaule *f* de porc

loin	longe *f* de porc
loin without bone in	longe *f* de porc sans os
sausages	saucisses *f*
chops	côtelettes *f* de porc
filet	filet *m* de porc
belly with bone in	poitrine *f* de porc
boneless belly	poitrine *f* de porc désossée
tenderloin	milieu *f* de filet de porc
spare rib	travers *m* de porc
loin chop	côtelette *f* de filet de porc
tenderloin	milieu *f* de filet de porc
round (slice)	rouelle *f* de porc
jaw	mâchoire *f* de porc
ear	oreille *f* de porc
cheek	joue *f* de porc
heart	coeur *m* de porc
kidney	rognon *m* de porc
rind	couenne *f* (de porc, de jambon)
chine	échine *f* de porc
potted head	fromage *m* de tête
brawn	fromage *m* d'italie, de cochon
knuckle; foreleg; hand	jambonneau *m*
chopped pieces of pork & fat	lardons *m* de porc
salt pork	petit salé
potted meat (duck, pork)	rillettes *f* (de canard; de porc)
poultry	volaille *f*

Q

quail — calle *f*
  quail's eggs — œufs *m* de caille

R

rabbit — lapin *m*
  young rabbit — lapereau *m*
  wild rabbit — lapin *m* de garenne
  rabbit legs — cuisses *f* de lapin
  rabbit legs minus the thighs — gigolettes *f* de lapin
  rabbit chopped into pieces — lapin *m* découpé
  saddle of rabbit — râble *m* de lapin
  rabbit's liver — foie *m* de lapin
reindeer — renne *m*
  saddle of reindeer — selle *f* de renne
  roe deer — chevrette *f* (see also *kid*)

S

salami — salami *m*
sausage(s) — saucisse(s) *f*
  preserved — saucisson *m*
  sausage meat — chair *f* à saucisse
  garlic sausage *(salami)* — saucisson *m* à l'ail
  dry cured sausage *(salami)* — saucisson *m* sec
  chipolata — chipolata *f*
  type of beef sausage — saucisses *f* de Strasbourg
  toulouse sausages — saucisses *f* de Toulouse

blood s'age, 'black pudding'	boudin *m* noir
blood s'age, 'white pudding'	boudin *m* blanc
sausage from chitterlings	andouille / andouillette *f*
saveloy	cervelas *m*
snails	escargots *m*
variety of snail	acave *f*
snipe	bécassine *f*
stuffing, forcemeat	farce *f*
sweetbreads	ris *m*

T
___

terrine (cooked potted meat, usually shredded)	terrine *f* see *pâté* e.g. terrine de canard
tongue	langue *f*
tournedos	see *beef*
tripe	tripe *f;* gras-double *m* cru
turkey	
female turkey	dinde *f*
male turkey	dindon *m*
young turkey	dindonneau *f*
legs of turkey	cuisses *f* de dinde
breast of turkey	blanc *m* de dinde
wing of turkey	aileron *m* dinde
turkey piece for stewing	blanquette *f* dinde

V

veal   veau *m*
   thick slice of veal   grenadin *m*
   fillet   rouelle *f* de veau
   neck of veal (for stewing)   collier *m* de veau
   rib of veal   côte de veau
   flank of veal   tendron *m* de veau
   knuckle   jarret *m* de veau
   collop   escalop *f* de veau
   calf's heart   coeur *m* de veau
   calf's liver   foie *m* de veau
   calf's head   tête *f* de veau
   calf's foot   pied *m* de veau
   calf's sweetbreads   ris *m* de veau
   stewing veal   blanquette *f* de veau
venison   chevreuil *m;* venaison *f*
   haunch of venison   quartier *m* de chevreuil

W

woodcock   bécasse *f*

Fruit and Vegetables

Fruits et Legumes

A

almonds	amandes *f*
anise/aniseed	anis *m* étoilé; badiane *f*
apples	
eating (desert)	pomme *f*
cooking	pomme *f* á cuir
apple sauce	compote *f* de pommes
apricot	abricot *m*
asparagus	
stick	une asperges *f*
bundle	botte *f* d'asperges
tips	pointe *f* d'asperges
artichokes	
Jerusalem	topinambour *m*
globe	artichaut *m*
heart	fond *m* d'artichaut
aubergine; egg plant	aubergine *f*

B

bananas	bananes *f*
barley	orge *f*
pearl barley	orge *f* perlé

basil	basilic *m*
bay leaf	feuille *f* de laurier
beans	
broad	(grosse) fèves
kidney, or haricot	haricots *m* nain; flageolets *m*
red	harricots *m* rouge
dried	haricots *m* secs
french	haricots *m* verts
runner	haricots *m* d'Espagne; haricots *m* grimpant
soya	pois *m* chinois
bean sprouts	pousse *f* de soja
beetroot	betterave *f*
white beet	blette *f*
bilberry	airelle *f*, myrtille *f*
blackberries	mûre *f*
black-currant	cassis *m,* raisin *m* de corinthe
blueberries	bluet *m*
boletus	bolet *m*
borage	bourrache *f*
broccoli - sprouting	brocoli *m*
broccoli - calabrese	brocoli *m*
brussels sprouts	choux *m* de bruxelles
buckwheat	blé noir *m*

C

cabbage	chou *m* (pl. *choux*)
savoy	chou *m* de milan
coleslaw	chou *m* blanc
chinese	chou *m* chinois
red	chou *m* rouge
green	chou *m* vert
curly kale	chou *m* frisé
sea kale	chou *m* marin
garden	chou *m* pommé
cardoons	cardon *m*
carrots	carottes *f*
cashew nut	noix *f* de cajou
cauliflowers	chou-fleurs *m*
celeriac	celeri-rave *m*
celery	celeri *m*
wild celery	ache *f* (de marais)
cherries	cerises *f*
morello cherries	griotte *f*
white-heart cherries	bigarreau *m*
chervil	cerfeuil *m*
chestnuts	châtaigne *f*; marrons *m*;
chickpeas	pois *m* chiches
chicory	chicorée *f* sauvage; endive *f*
chillis - red	piment *m* rouge
chillis - green	piment *m* vert
chives	ciboulette *f*

citrus fruit	agrume *m*
clementines	clémentines *f*
cloves	clou *m* de girofle
coconut	noix *f* de coco
comice pear	doyenné *m* du comice
coriander	coriandre *f*
corn cob (ear)	épi *m* de maïs
crab apple	pomme *f* sauvage
cranberry	airelle *f* coussinette
cress	cresson *m*, alénois *m*
cucumber - ridge	concombre *m*
cucumber - black	agoursi *m*
currants	raisin *m* de corinthe
currants - red	cassis *m;* groseille *f* rouge
currants - white	groseille *f* blanche

D

damsons	prunes *f* de damas
dates	dattes *f*
dill	aneth *m*

E

eggplant	see *aubergine*
endives	chicoree *f* frisee

F

fennel	fenouil *m*
fennel florence (giant)	férule *f*
figs	figues *f*
fruit	fruit *m*
wild berries	fruit *m* de bois
fresh fruit	fruit *m* frais
dried fruit	fruit *m* secs

G

garlic	ail *m*
spanish garlic	rocambole *f*
clove of garlic	gousse *f* d'ail
	caieu *m* d'ail
garlic sauce	aillade *f*
garlic with mayonnaise	aillolie *f*
gherkin	cornichon *m*
ginger - root / fresh	gingembre *m* frais
gooseberries	groseille *f* a maquereau
	groseille *f* verte
grapes	
dessert grapes	raisins *m* du table
bunch of grapes	grappe *f* de raisin
grapefruit	pamplemousse *m*
greengage	reine-claude *f*
grenadine	grenadine *f*

H

haricot beans	see *beans*
hazelnuts	noisette *f*
horseradish	raifort *m*

J

Jerusalem artichoke	see *artichoke*
juniper berry	genièvre *m*

K

kale	chou *m*
kale - curly	chou *m* frise
	chou *m* rouge
kidney bean	haricots *m* nain
	flageolets *m*
kidney beans - red	harricots *m* rouge
kiwi fruit	kiwis *m*
kohl-rabi	chou-rave *m*
	(pl. choux-raves)

L

lemon	citron *m*
leeks	poireau *m* (pl. poireaux)
lentil	lentille *f*

lettuce
    green lettuce   laitue *f*
    cabbage lettuce   laitue *f* pommée
    cos lettuce   laitue *f* romaine
    lamb's lettuce   mâche *f*
    oak leaf lettuce   feuille *f* de chêne
loganberry - see *peas*   ronce-framboise *f*

M

medlar   nèfle *f*
mango   mangue *f*
marjoram   marjolaine *f*
marrow   courge *f*; moelle *f*
    zucchini; courgette   courgette *f*
melon   melon *m*
    water melon   pastéque *f*
mint   menthe *f*
mulberries   mûres *f*
mushrooms   champignons *m*
    boletus   bolet *m*
    cepe   cèpe *m*
    chanterelle grey   chanterelle *f* gris;
    modeste *f* chanterelle yellow   chanterelle *f* jaune
    girolles   girolles *f*
    morel   morille *f*
    milk cap   lactaires *f*
    fairy ring   mousserons *m*

paris bleu	paris *m* bleu
chestnut	paris *m* brun
bluefoot; wood bluets	pieds *m* bleu
hedgehog	pieds *m* de mouton
trumpets of death	trompettes *f* de la morte
mustard and cress	moutarde *f* blanche et cresson alénois

N

nectarine	nectarine *f*; brugnon *m*
nutmeg	noix *f* de muscade

O

oats	avoine *f*
olives	olives *f*
onions	oignons *m*
spring onions	ciboule *f*
string of onions	chapelet *m* d'oignons
origano	origan *m*

P

parsley	persil *m*
parsnips	panais *m*
peaches	pêches *f*
peanut / peanuts	cacahuète *f* clopinettes *f*

pears	poires *f*
peas	
green peas	petit pois *m*
split peas	pois *m* cassés
sugar peas	mange-tout *m*
peppers - sweet red	piment *m* doux;
	poivrons *m* capiscum *m*
persimmon	kaki *m*
pineapple	ananas *m*
pistachio nut	pistache *f*
plantain	plantain *m*
plums	prunes *f*
type of plum	mirabelle *f*
pomegranate	grenade *f*
prunes	pruneaux *f*
potatoes	pommes *f* de terre
baking	pommes *f* de terre au four
new	pommes *f* de terre nouvelles
pumpkin	citrouille *f;* potiron *m*
puy lentils	lentilles *f* vert du puy

Q

quince	coing *m*

R

raisins	raisins *m* sec
radishes	radis *m*
raspberries	framboises *f*
red cabbage - see *cabbage*	
red currants - see *currants*	
rhubarb	rhubarbe *f*
rocket	roquette *f*
rosemary	romarin *m*
runner beans	haricot *m* d'Espagne; haricot *m* grimpant

S

sage	sauge *f*
salsify	salsifis *m*
sauerkraut	choucroute *f*
savory	sarriette *f*
scorzoneras	scorsonère *f;* salsifis noir
seakale	crambe *m*; crambé *m*; chou marin
shallots	chalote *f*
sloes	prunelles *f*
sorrel	oseille *f*
soya beans - see *beans*	
spinach - leaf	épinards *m* en branche
spinach - puree	épinards *m* purée (usually frozen)
sprouting seeds	luzerne *f*
strawberries	fraises *f*

wild strawberries	fraises *f* du bois
swedes	rutabaga *m;* navet *m* de suède
sweetcorn	maïs *m* doux
sweet potato	patate *f* douce
Swiss chard	blette *f* (sometimes 'bette')

T

tangerine	mandarine *f*
tarragon	estragon *m*
thyme	thym *m*
wild thyme	serpolet *m*
tomatoes	tomates *f*
truffles	truffe *f*
turnips	navets *m*

U

ugli	aeglé *m*

W

walnuts	noix *f*
walnut halves	cerneaux de noix *f*
watercress	cresson *m* de fontaine
wheat	blé *m;* froment *m*
white beet	poirée *f*

Y

yam	igname *f*
yarrow - wild	achilléeé *f*

Fish and Shellfish

Fruits de Mer

A

albacore   liche *f*
anchovy   anchois *m*
angler fish, *aka* monkfish,   baudroie *f;* lotte *f*
frogfish, sea-devil

B

barracuda   barracuda *m*
bass - sea bass   loup *m* de mer; bar *m*
black pollock   lieu *m* noir
bloater   hareng bouffi *m* ; craquelot *m*
bonito   bonite *f*
bream - freshwater   brème *f*
bream - sea bream   dorade *f;* acarne *f*
brill   barbue *f;* sandre *f*

C

calamari   calmar *m; encornet *m*
carp   carpe *f*
catfish   poisson-chat *m*
caviare   caviar *m*

chub	chabot *m*
clams	palourdes *f*; praires *f*
coalfish	coalie *f*
cockle	coque *f*; boucarde (bucarde) *f*; clovisse *f*
cod - fresh	cabillaud *m*
cod - slice/slab	darne *f*
cod - salted	morue *f* seche
cod - roe	laitance *f* du cabillaud; laitance *f* de morue
coley	lieu *m*
conger eel	congre *m*; anguille *f* de mer
crab	crabe *m*
crabmeat	chair *f* de crabe
crayfish - freshwater	écrevisse *f*
a crustacean	alphée *f*
cuttlefish	seiche *f*

D

dogfish	chien *m* de mer

E

eels	anguilles *f*
conger eel	anguilles *f* de mer
escallop - see *scallop*	

F

flounder	flet *m*
fry	alevin *m*

G

garfish	orphie *f*
grayling	ombre *m*
grouper	mérou *m*
gudgeon	gujon *m*
gurnard or gurnet - red	grondin *m* rouge
gurnard or gurnet - grey	grondin *m* gris

H

haddock - fresh	aiglefin *m*
haddock - smoked	haddock *m*
hake	colin *m;* merluche *f*
halibut	flétan *m*
herrings	harengs *m*
herrings - red	harengs *m* saurs
hog-fish (scorpion-fish)	rascasse *f*

J

John Dory	St. Pierre *m*; doré *m* (jean)

L

lamprey	lamproie *f*

langoustine	langoustine *f*
lemon sole	limande *f*; sole *f* limande
ling	lingue *f*; morue longue
lobster	homard *m*
lobster soup	bisque *f* d'homard

M

mackerel	maquereau *m*
grey mullet	mulet *m*
red mullet	rouget *m*
monkfish aka angler fish, frog-fish, sea-devil	lotte *f;* baudroie *f*
mussels	moules *f*

O

octopus	poulpe *m*
oysters	huîtres *f*

P

perch	perche *f*
type of perch	aceline *f*
pike	brochet *m*
pilchards	pilchards *m*
plaice	plie *f;* carrelet *m*
pollack	merlan *m* jaune; lieu *m* noir
pout - see *whiting*	tacaud *m*

prawns	crevettes *f* rose
jumbo prawns	gambas *f*
also called *coalfish*	rousette *f*

S

saithe - see also *pollack*	lieu *m* noir
salmon	saumon *m*
slice/slab of salmon	darne *f*
salmon trout - aka *sea trout*	truite *f* saumonée
sardines	sardines *f*
scallop	coquille *f* Saint Jacques; escallops *f*
scampi	langoustines *f*
scorpion-fish - see *hog-fish*	rascasse *f*
sea bass	loup *m* de mer; bar *m*
sea anemone	actinie *f*
sea urchin	oursin *m*
shad	alose *f*
shark	peau *f* bleu
shrimps	crevettes *f* grise
skate	raie *f*
fish similar to skate	torpille *f*
smelts	éperlan *m;* (pl. poissons des chenaux)
smoked salmon	saumon *m* fumée
soft roe	laitance *f*
sole	sole *f*

sprats	sprat *m* ; harenguets *m*
spider crab	arraignée *f* de mer
squid; calamari	encornet *m*
sturgeon	esturgeon *m*
swordfish	espadon *m*

T

tench	tanche *f*
trout	truite *f*
turbot	turbot *m*
tuna	thon *m*

W

whale	baleine *f*
whelks	buccins *m*
whitebait	blanchailles *f*
whiting	merlan *m;* tacaud *m*
wing of skate	côte *f* de raie
winkle	bigorneau *m*

Y

yellow pollock	lieu *m* jaune

Dairy and Bakery

Boulangerie

B

baking soda	bicarbonate *m* de soude
baking powder	levure *f* chimique
biscuit	biscuit *m*
crisp - served with ice cream	biscotin *m*
cracker	biscuit *m* salé;
	biscuit *m* dur
sponge finger	biscuit *m* à la cuillère
ginger	biscuit *m* au gingembre
shortbread	sablé *m*
macaroon	macaron *m*
wafer	gaufrette *f*
bread	pain *m*
loaf of bread	miche *f* de pain
stick	baguette *f*
long thin loaf of bread	flûte *f*
plaited loaf of bread	tresse *f* de pain
roll	petit pain *m*
crescent-shaped roll	croissant *m*
soft bread; bread roll	pain *m* mollet
cream bun	chou *m* à la crème

soft, sweet, light, doughy	brioche *f*
large bun	
slice of bread	tranche *f* de pain
breadcrumbs	chapelures *f*
bagel	petit pain *m* en couronne
brown bread	pain *m* complet; pain *m* bis
farmhouse bread	pain *m* de campagne
rye bread	pain *m* de siegle
sandwich bread	pain *m* de mie
wheat bread	pain *m* de froment
soda bread	pain *m* au bicarbonate de soude
walnut bread	pain *m* aux noix
white bread	pain *m* blanc
wholemeal bread	pain *m* complet
roll with chocolate filling	pain *m* au chocolat
roll with raisins	pain *m* aux raisins
dry toast	biscotte *f*
croutons	croûtons *m*
unsalted bread	pain *m* sans sel
butter	beurre *m*
slightly salted butter	beurre *m* demi sel
unsalted butter	beurre *m* sans sel

C

cake	gateau *m* (pl. gateaux)
cheesecake	tarte *f* au fromage blanc parfumée au citron

fruit cake	cake *m*
gingerbread cake	pain *m* d'épice
slab of gingerbread	pavé *m*
sponge cake	génoise *f;* biscuit *m* de savoie
swiss roll	bûche *f* de noël
oat cake	galette *f* d'avoine
pancake	galette *f*
small cakes	pâtisserie *f* légère; gateaux *m;* pâtisseries *f*
cheese straws (fingers)	biscuit *m* fourrè au fromage
éclair	éclair *m*
cheese	fromage *m*
cows milk cheese	fromage *m* de vache
goats milk cheese	fromage *m* de chèvre
cream cheese	fromage *m* à la crème; fromage *m* à tartiner; petit suisse
processed cheese	fromage *m* fondu; fromage *f* industriel
low fat cheese	fromage *m* maigre; fromage *m* blanc
soft cheese enriched with cream	fromage *m* frais
cream	crème *f*
double cream	crème *f* fraîche
single cream	crème *f* fraîche liquide
light (thin) cream	crème *f* légère

half cream	crème *f* semi epaisse
low fat cooking cream	crème *f* fleurette
ice cream	glace *f*
soured cream	crème *f* aigre
clotted cream	crème *f* caillée (par échaudage)
whipped cream	crème *f* fouettée; crème chantilly
custard	crème *f* au lait

D

doughnuts	beignets *m*

E

egg(s)	œuf *f* (pl. des œufs)

F

flour	farine *f*
cornflour	farine *f* de maïs
wheat flour	farine *f* de blé; fleur de farine *f*
wholemeal	farine *f* complet
oatmeal	farine *f* d'avoine
self-raising flour	farine *f* préparée à la levure chimique
pastry flour	farine *f* pâtissière
rye flour	farine *f* de siegle
fruit cake - see *cake*	

M

margarine margarene *f*
marzipan massepain *m*
meringue meringue *f*
milk

cow's milk	lait *m*
goat's milk	lait *m* de chèvre
full cream	lait *m*entier
skimmed milk	lait *m* écrémés
emi-skimmed milk	lait *m* demi-écrémé
long life, uht	lait *m* longue conservation; lait *m* homogénéisé(e)
condensed milk	lait *m* concentré sucré
powdered milk	lait *m* en poudre
evaporated milk	lait *m* concentré
baby milk	lait *m* pour le bébé
milk for a growing child	lait *m* croissance
malted milk	farine *f* lactée
buttermilk	babeurre *m*
curdled milk	caillé *f*
curds	caillebotte *f*
rennet	caillette *f*

P

pastry	pâtisserie *f*; pâte *f*
croissant	croissant *m*
puff pastry	pâte *f* feuiletée
puff pastry roll with	chausson *m* au
apple filling	pommes sablée
pastry	pâte *f* sablée
shortcrust pastry	pâte *f* brisée
thin rolled (base for cakes or tart)	abaisse *f*

S

scones	pains *m* au lait

T

tart	tarte *f*
small tart	tartelette *f*

Y

yeast	levure *f*
yoghurt	yaourt *m;* yoghourt *m*

Z

zabaglione	sabayon *m*

Wines and Spirits

Vins et Spiritueux

A

apricot brandy	abricotine *f*
apple brandy	calvados *m*
armagnac	armagnac *m*

B

beer	bière *f*
blackcurrant liqueur	cassis, crème de
brandy	
apricot brandy	abricotine *f*
apple brandy	calvados *m*
fruit brandy	eau *f* de vie
liqueur brandy	fine champagne *f*
burgundy	vin *m* de bourgoigne

C

champagne	champagne *f*
cider	cidre *m*
claret	vin *m* de bordeaux
dry; unsweetened	brut

F

fruit brandy   eau *f* de vie

G

gin   gin *m*

L

liquer brandy   fine champagne *f*
liqueur - peppermint-flavoured   crème *f* de menthe
liqueur - sweet cocoa-flavoured   crème *f* de cacao
locality of a vinyard   cru *m*

P

port   porto *m*

R

rosé wine   vin *m* rosé

S

sherry   xérès *m*

T

tonic water   eau *f* tonique

W

water - still	eau *f* naturelle
water - sparkling	eau *f* gaseuse
water - drinkable	eau *f* potable
wine of the first growth	vin *m* de premiè cuvée

Grocery and Spices

Épiceries

A

allspice	piment *m* de la Jamaïque
american seasoning	bbq *m*
angelica	angélique
apricot juice	jus *m* d,abricot
aniseed	anis *m*
aspic jelly	aspic *m*

B

baked beans	haricots *m* verts à la sauce tomate
baker's yeast	levure *f* de boulangerie
baking powder	levure *f* chimique
basil	basilic *m*
beer	bière *f*
birds eye chillies	langues *f* d'oiseau
bread-crumbs - for frying	chapelure *f*
buckwheat	sarrasin *m;* blé *m* noir

C

capers	câpres *f*

capers in brine	câpres *f* à l'eau salé
caraway seeds	graines *f* de carvi
cardamon whole	cardamom *m*
caster sugar	sucre *f* semoule
cayenne pepper	poivre *f* de cayenne
celery salt	sel *m* de céleri
cereals - breakfast	céréals *f* en flocon
chestnuts in syrup	marrons *m* glacé
chicken seasoning	poulet *m*
chick-peas	pois *m* chiche
chili powder hot	poudre *f* de chili fort
chili powder mild	poudre *f* de chili mi-fort
chillies crushed	piment *m* concassé
chives	ciboulette *f*
chocolate for cooking	chocolat *m* à cuir
cinnamon ground	cannelle *f* moulue
cinnamon sticks	cannelle *f* en batons
citrus fruit jam	confiture *f* d'agrumes
cloves - ground	clous *m* de girofle moulue
cloves - whole	clous *m* de girofle entier
compote (puree) of fruit	marmelade *f*
cooking salt	sel *m* culinaire
cinnamon	cannelle *f*
coarse ground white pepper	mignonette *f*
cocoa	cacao *m*
coffee	café *m*
coffee - roasted	café *m* torréfié

coffee beans	grains *m* de café
coriander ground	coriandre *f* moulue
coriander leaf	coriandre *f*
coriander	graines *f* de coriandre
cornflour	bleuet *m;* barbeau *m*
cumin seed ground	cumin *m* en poudre
cumin seed whole	graines *f* de cumin
curry powder	curry / cari *m*

D

dill weed	aneth *m*
dijon mustard	moutarde *f* de dijon

F

fat - lard	gras(se) *m*; graisse *f*
fat - pork	gras *m* de porc
fat - duck	gras *m* de canard
fat - goose	gras *m* d'oie
fennel seed	graines *f* de fenouil
fenugreek	fenugrec *m*
fenugreek ground	fenugrec *m* en poudre
fish seasoning	poisson *m*
fish soup	soupe *f* de poisson
fish soup sauce	sauce *f* rouille
fondant chocolate	chocolat *m* fondant
fruit juice	jus *m* de fruit

G

garam masala	garam masala
garlic	ail *m*
garlic granules	ail *m* en poudre
garlic minced	ail *m* haché
gelatine	gélatine *f*
ginger ground	gingembre *m* mouloue
grape seed oil	huile *f* de raisin
grasswort	salicorne *f*
grated cheese	fromage *f* rapé
groundnut oil	huile *f* d' arachide

H

hazel nut oil	huile *f* de noisette
herb mixture of chopped chives chervil, parsley, tarragon (dried)	fines herbes *f*
herbes de provence	herbes *f* de provence
honey	miel *m*
horseradish sauce	sauce *f* au raifort

I

ice cream	glace *f*

J

jam, preserve(s)	confiture *f*

jelly	gelée *f*
juniper berries	baies *f* de genièvre
juniper berry jam	confiture *f* de genièvre

L

lamb seasoning	agneau *m*

M

mace	macis *m;* fleur *f* de muscade
mace - ground	macis *m* en poudre
macaroni	macaroni *m*
marjoram	marjolaine *f*
marmalade - orange	confiture *f* d'oranges
marmalade - lemon	confiture *f* de citrons
marzipan	massepain *m*
mineral water - still	eau *f* minérale naturelle
mineral water - sparkling	eau *f* minérale naturelle gazeuse
mint	menthe *f*
mixed spices	melange d'épices *f*
mustard	moutarde *f*
mustard seed	moutarde *f* en graine

N

noodles, spaghetti, etc.	pâtes *f* alimentaires; des nouilles *f*

nutmeg	noix *f* de muscade
ground nutmeg	noix *f* de muscade mouloue

O

olive oil	huile *f* d'olive
olive oil - virgin/first pressing	huile *f* d'olive virgine
onion salt	sel *m* d'oignon
orange juice	jus *m* d'orange
oregano	origan *m*

P

paprika	paprika *m*
parmesan	parmesan *m*
parsley	persil *m*
pastry case, scallop-shaped	pétoncle *m*
pepper	poivre *m*
black and red pepper	poivre *m* noir et rouge
black ground pepper	poivre *m* noir mouloue
black coarse ground pepper	poivre *m* concassé
lemon pepper	poivre *m* au citron
white ground pepper	poivre *m* blanc mouloue
peppercorns	grains *m* de poivre
tropical mixed peppercorns	melange poivres *m* des tropiques
potato starch	fécule *f* de pommes de terre
potted meat, cooked & shredded (pork, duck, game, chicken)	rillettes *f*

Q

quince   coing *m*

R

rapeseed oil   huile *f* de colza

S

saffron   safran *m*
sage   sauge *m*
salt   sel *m*
  coarse salt   sel *m* gros
  fine salt   sel *m* fin
  sea salt   sel *m* de mer
semolina   semoule *f*
sesame seed   sesame *f*
shellfish soup   bisque *f*
soya bean oil   huile *f* de soja
soy sauce   sauce *f* soja
spaghetti (see *noodles* above)   pâtes *f* alimentaires
spices   épice *f*
stock - liquid or cubes   bouillon *m* (liquide de
                                        cuisson, *or* concentré)

stoned olives   olives *f* dénoyautée
stuffed olives   olives *f* farci
sunflower oil   huile *f* de tournesol

sugar   sucre *m*
  brown sugar   sucre *m* roux
  soft brown sugar   cassonade *f*

T

table salt   sel *m* blanc
tarragon   estragon *m*
tea   thé *m*
thyme   thym *m*
tomato juice   jus *m* de tomates
tomato ketchup   sauce *f* piquante (en
                                          bouteille) à base de
                                          tomates

truffle oil   huile *f* de truffe
turmeric   safran *m* des indes

V

vanilla   vanille *f*
  vanilla essence   extrait *m* de vanille
  vanilla pod   cosse *f* de vanille
vegetable oil   huile *f* de vegetale
vermicelli   vermicelles f
vinegar   vinaigre *m*
  cider vinegar   vinaigre *m* du cidre
  wine vinegar   vinaigre *m* de vin
  malt vinegar   vinaigre *m* de malt
vinegrette - hazelnut   vinaigre *m* de noisette

Viand, Gibier et Volailles

Meat, Game and Poultry

A

abats *m*	giblets
acave *f*	variety of snail
agneau *m*	lamb
agneau de lait	suckling lamb
aiguillette *f*	thin slice of the breast of poultry
aile *f*	breast on the bone, wing
aileron *m* **dinde**	wing of turkey
aloyau *m* **de bœuf** (pl. aloyaux)	sirloin of beef
andouille / andouillette *f*	sausage made of chitterlings

B

bavette *f*	flank of beef
bavette *f* **aloyau de bœuf à bifteck**	top side of sirloin of beef
bécasse *f*	woodcock
bécassine *f*	snipe
blanc *m* **de dinde**	turkey breast
blanc *m* **de volaille**	chicken breast
blanc *m* **d'oie**	goose breast

blanquette *f* **dinde**	turkey pieces for stewing
blanquette *f* **de veau**	stewing veal
bœuf *m*	beef
bœuf *m* **à faire cuire en ragoût**	stewing steak
bœuf *m* **à faire frire**	frying steak
bœuf *m* **à cuire en daube**	braising steak
boudin *m* **noir**	blood sausage, 'black pudding'
boudin *m* **blanc**	blood sausage, 'white pudding'

C

caille *f*	quail
canard *m*	duck
canard *m* **fumé**	smoked duck
canard *m* **sauvage**	wild duck
canard *m* **siffleur**	widgeon
canard *m* **sarcelle**	teal
caneton *m*	male duck, duckling
canette *f*	female duck
carcasse *f*	carcass
carré *f* **d'agneau**	rack of lamb
cervelas *m*	saveloy
chair *f* **à saucisse**	sausage meat
chapon *m*	capon
chèvre *f*	goat

chevreau *m*	kid
chevrette *f*	she-goat; roe deer
chevreuil *m*	roe deer (male)
chipolata *f*	chipolata
cochon *m*	pig
cœur *m* **d'agneau**	lamb's heart
cœur *m* **de porc**	pig's heart
cœur *m* **de poulet**	chicken heart
cœur *m* **de veau**	calf's heart
cochon *m* **de lait**	suckling pig
collet *m* **d'agneau**	best end of neck of lamb
collet *m* **de mouton**	scrag of mutton
collier *m* **de bœuf**	neck of beef
collier *m* **de veau**	neck of veal (for stewing)
colvet *m*	mallard
confit *m* e.g. **de canard**	conserve (e.g. of duck)
coq *m* de **bruyère**	capercailze
coquelet *m*	young cockerel
côte *f* **d'agneau**	rib of lamb
côte *f* **de bœuf**	rib of beef
côte *f* **de veau**	rib of veal
côte *f* **filet d'agneau**	undercut of lamb
côte *f* **d'aloyau**	wing rib of beef
côte première de bœuf *m*	loin chop - beef
côtelette *f* **d'agneau**	lamb chop
côtelette *f* **de filet de porc**	loin chop - pork
côtelettes *f* **de porc**	pork chops

côtelettes *f* **de volaille**	chicken cutlets
côtes *f* **découvertes**	middle neck cutlets of lamb
couenne *f* **de porc**	pork rind
cuisses *f* **de canard**	duck legs
cuisses *f* **de dinde**	turkey legs
cuisses *f* **de grenouilles**	frog's legs
cuisses *f* **de lapin**	rabbit legs
cuisses *f* **de volaille**	chicken legs
cuisses *f* **d'oie**	goose legs
culotte *f* **de bœuf**	rump or buttock of beef

D

dinde *f*	turkey female
dindon *m*	turkey male
dindonneau *f*	young turkey

E

entrecôte *f*	entrecote steak
épaule *f* **d'agneau**	shoulder of lamb
épaule *f* **d'agneau semi désossée**	shoulder of lamb half-boned
épaule *f* **de bœuf**	shoulder of beef
épaule *f* **de porc**	shoulder of pork
éscalope *f* **de veau**	collop of veal
éscargots *m*	snails
échine *f* **de porc**	chine of pork

F

farce *f*	stuffing, forcemeat
faisan *m* **cock**	cock pheasant
faisane *f* **hen**	hen pheasant
faux-fillet *m*; **biftek** *m* **dans l'aloyau**	sirloin steak
fermier	free range (poultry)
filet *m* **de bœuf, tournedos** *m*	fillet steak
filet *m* **de porc**	fillet of pork
filet *m* **mignon**	cut from the small end of fillet of beef; undercut from saddle of lamb/mutton
flanchet *m* **de bœuf**	flank of beef
foie *m* **d'agneau**	lamb's livers
foie *m* **de cochon (porc)**	pig's liver
foie *m* **de lapin**	rabbit's liver
foies *m* **de volaille**	chicken liver
fois *m* **de veau**	calf's liver
fois *m* **(pl. foies)**	liver
fromage *m* **de cochon**	brawn
fromage *m* **d'italie**	brawn
fromage *m* **de tête**	potted head

G

gésiers *m*	gizzards
gibier *m*	game
gigolettes *f* **de lapin**	rabbit legs minus thighs

51

gigot *m* **d'agneau**	leg of lamb
gigot *m* **d'agneau raccourci**	half a leg of lamb
gîte *m* **à la noix**	silverside of beef
gras-double *m* **cru**	tripe
grenadin *m*	thick slice of veal
grouse *m*	grouse

H

haché *m* **d'agneau**	minced lamb
haché *m* **de bœuf**	minced beef
hampe *f* **de boeuf**	flank of beef

J

jambon *m*	ham
jambon *m*	leg of pork
jambon *m* **couenne**	cokked ham with rind
jambon *m* **cuit**	cooked ham
jambon *m* **de parme**	parma ham
jambon *m* **de pays**	dry cured ham
jambonneau *m*	knuckle ; foreleg ; hand of pork
jarret *m* **d'agneau**	lambshank
jarret *m* **de bœuf**	shin of beef
avec os	shin of beef with bone
sans os	shin of beef without bone
jarret *m* **de veau**	knuckle of veal
joue *f* **de porc**	pig's cheek

L

langue *f* **de bœuf**	ox tongue
langue *f* **de porc**	pig's tongue
lapereau *m*	young rabbit
lapin *m*	rabbit
lapin *m* **de garenne**	wild rabbit
lapin *m* **découpé**	rabbit chopped into pieces
lard *m*	bacon unsliced
lard *m* **fumé**	smoked bacon
lard *m* **entrelardé**	streaky bacon
lard *m* **maigre**	lean bacon
lardons *m* **en tranche**	bacon rashers
lardons *m* **de porc**	pieces of pork meat and fat chopped small
levraut	leveret
lièvre *m*	hare
longe *f* **de porc**	loin of pork
sans os	loin of pork without bone

M

macreuse *f* **de boeuf**	lean meat from a shoulder of beef
magret *m* **de canard**	breast of duck
maigre	lean meat
maigre de porc	lean pork

marcassin *m* — young wild boar
mâchoire *f* **de porc** — pig's jaw
milieu *f* **de filet de porc** — tenderloin of pork
moelle *f* — bone marrow
mou *m* — lights
mousse *f* (e.g. de canard) — paté (e.g.duck)
mouton *m* — mutton

O

œufs *m* **de caille** — quail's eggs
œufs *m* **de mouette** — gull's eggs
œufs *m* **de vanneau** — plover's eggs
oie *f* — goose
oie *f* **fumé** — smoked goose
onglet *m* **(de boeuf)** — prime cut of beef
oreille *f* **de porc** — pig's ear
os *m* **à moelle** — marrow bone
ortolan *m* — ortolan

P

paleron *m* **de bœuf** — chuck of beef
pâté *m* — meat paste, usually smooth, usually served cold, made from pork, duck, goose, chicken, game, etc.

pâté *m* **de fois de canard**	duck liver pate
pâté *m* **de fois de volaille**	chicken liver pate
pâté *m* **de fois gras**	goose liver pate
pâté *m* **forestière**	pate with mushrooms
pâte *m* **de gibier**	game pie
perdrix *f* (pl. perdreau)	partridge
petit salé	salt pork
piece *f* **parée de bœuf à bifteck**	piece of steak trimmed
pieds *m* **de cochon (porc)**	pig's trotters
pieds *m* **de porc cru**	pig's trotters - uncooked
pieds *m* **de mouton**	sheep trotters
pieds *m* **de veau**	calf's feet
pigeon *m*	pigeon
pigeon *m* **ramier**	wood pigeon
pigeonneau *m*	young pigeon; squab
pintade *f*	guinea fowl
pintadeau(x) *m*	young guinea fowl
plumé	plucked
poitrine *f* **d'agneau**	breast of lamb
poitrine *f* **de bœuf**	brisket of beef
poitrine *f* **de bœuf avec os à rotir**	brisket of beef with bone to roast
poitrine *f* **de bœuf sans os à bouiller**	brisket of beef without bone to boil
poitrine *f* **de porc avec os**	pork belly with bone
poitrine *f* **de porc désossée**	pork belly without bone
porc *m*	pork

porcelet *m*	suckling pig
(see *cochon de lait* above)	
poularde *f*	fattened chicken
poulet *m*	chicken
poule *f*	boiling chicken
poulet *m* **fumé**	smoked chicken
poulet *m* **de grain**	corn fed chicken
poussin *m*	young chicken
préparé pour rôtir	trussed

Q

quartier *m* **de chevreuil**	haunch of venison

R

râble *m* **de lapin**	saddle of rabbit
râble *m* **de lièvre**	saddle of hare
renne *m*	reindeer
rillettes *f*	potted shredded meat
(e.g. d'oie; de canard; de porc)	(e.g goose; duck; pork)
ris *m*	sweetbreads
ris *m* **d'agneau**	sweetbreads (lamb)
ris *m* **de veau**	sweetbreads (calf)
rognon *m*	kidney
rognon *m* **d'agneau**	lamb's kidney
rognon *m* **de porc**	pig's kidney
rouelle *f* **de bœuf**	round (slice) of beef

rouelle *f* **de porc**	round (slice) of pork
rouelle *f* **de veau**	fillet of veal
rumsteck *m*	rump steak
rumsteck *m* **bœuf aiguillette**	slice of rump steak

S

salami *m*	salami saussage
sanglier *m*	wild boar
sarcelle *f*	teal
saucisse(s) *f*	sausage(s) uncooked
saucisson *m* **à l'ail**	garlic salami sausage
saucisson *m* **sec**	cooked dried salami sausage
saucisses *f* **de Strasbourg**	type of beef sausage
saucisses *f* **de Toulouse**	toulouse saussages
saucisson *m*	preserved, dry sausage
selle *f* **d'agneau**	saddle of lamb
selle *f* **de mouton**	saddle of mutton
selle *f* **de renne**	saddle of reindeer
siffleur *m*	widgeon

T

tende *f* **de tranche de bœuf**	topside of beef
tendron *m* **de veau**	flank of veal
terrine *f* (see also *pâté* above)	cooked potted meat, usually shredded

tête *f* **de cochon**	pig's head
tête *f* **de mouton**	sheep's head
tête *f* **de veau**	calf's head
tétras *m*	grouse (see also *grouse*)
tranche *f* **de bacon**	a rasher of bacon
tranche *f* **de magret de canard** fumée et seche	slice of breast of duck, smoked and dried
tranche *f* **gigot d'agneau** avec os	slice of leg of lamb with bone in
tranche *f* **gigot d'agneau** sans os	slice of leg of lamb without bone
travers *m* **de porc**	spare rib of pork
tripe *f*	tripe

V

vanneau *m*; **pluvier** *m*	plover
veau *m*	veal
venaison *f*	venison
viande *f* **de cheval**	horse meat
viande *f* **hachée**	minced meat
vidé et paré	drawn and prepared
volaille *f*	poultry; fowl

Legumes et Fruit

Vegetables and Fruit

A

abricot *m*	apricot
ache *f* **(de marais)**	wild celery
achillée *f*	wild yarrow
aeglé *m*	ugli
agoursi *m*	ridge cucumber
agrume *m*	citrus fruit
ail *m*	garlic
aillade *f*	garlic sauce
aillolie *f*	garlic and mayonnaise
airelle *f*	bilberry
airelle *f* **coussinette**	cranberry
(see also *coussinette*)	
alénois *m*	garden cress
amandes *f*	almonds
ananas *m*	pineapple
aneth *m*	dill
anis *m* (see also *badiane*)	aniseed
anis *m* **étoilé**	star anise
artichaut *m*	globe artichoke
asperge *f*	asparagus

aubergine *f*	aubergine; egg plant
avoine *f*	oats

B

badiane *m* (see also *anis étoilé*)	aniseed / star anise
baie *f* **rouge**	cranberry
bananes *f*	bananas
basilic *m*	basil
bette *f* (see *blette*)	swiss chard
betterave *f*	beetroot
bigarreau *m*	white-heart cherry
blé *m* (see also *froment*)	wheat
blé noir *m*	buckwheat
blette *f* (alternative spelling)	swiss chard
bluet *m*	blueberries
bolet *m*	boletus mushroom
botte *f* **d'asperges**	asparagus bundle
bourrache *f*	borage
brocoli *m*	broccoli
brocoli *m*	calabrese
brugnon *m*	nectarine

C

cacahuète *f* (see also *clopinettes*)	peanut
caieu *m* **d'ail**	clove of garlic
capiscum *m*	sweet pepper

cardon *m*	cardoons
carottes *f*	carrots
cassis *m*	blackcurrant
(see also *raisin de corinthe*)	
celeri *m*	celery
celeri-rave *m*	celeriac
cèpe	boletus mushroom
cerfeuil *m*	chervil
cerises *f*	cherries
cerneaux de noix *f*	half walnuts
champignons *m*	mushrooms
chanterelle *f* **gris**	small, grey, edible
(see also *modeste*)	mushroom
chanterelle *f* **jaune**	small, yellow,
	edible mushroom
chapelet *m* **d'oignons**	string of onions
châtaigne *f* (see also *marrons*)	chestnuts
chicorée *f* **sauvage** (see also *endive*)	chicory broad leaf
chicorée *f* **frisee**	endives curled
chou *m*	kale
chou *m* (pl. choux)	cabbage
chou *m* **blanc**	coleslaw
chou *m* **chinois**	chinese cabbage
chou *m* **frisé**	curly kale
chou *m* **marin** (see also *crambé*)	sea kale
chou *m* **de milan**	savoy cabbage
chou *m* **pommé**	garden cabbage

chou *m* **rouge**	red cabbage; scotch kale
chou *m* **vert**	green cabbage
choucroute *f*	sauerkraut
chou-fleurs *m*	cauliflowers
chou-rave *m* (pl. *choux-raves*)	kohl-rabi
choux *m* **de bruxelles**	brussels sprouts
ciboule *f*	spring onion
ciboulette *f*	chives
citron *m*	lemon
citrouille *f* (see also *poitron*)	pumpkin
clémentines *f*	clementines
clopinettes *f* (see also *cacahuète*)	peanuts
clou *m* **de girofle**	cloves
coing *m*	quince
compote *f* **de pommes**	apple sauce
concombre *m*	cucumber
coriandre *f*	coriander
cornichon *m*	gherkin
courge *f*	marrow
courgette *f*	zucchini
coussinette *f* (see also *airelle coussinette*)	cranberry
crambé *m* (see also *chou marin*)	seakale
cresson *m*	cress
cresson *m* **de fontaine**	watercress

D

dattes *f*	dates
doyenné *m* **du comice**	comice pear

E

échalote *f*	shallots
endive *f* (see also *chicory sauvage*)	chicory broad leaf
épi *m* **de maïs**	corn cob (ear)
épinards *m* **en branche**	spinach leaf
épinards *m* **purée**	spinach puree
estragon *m*	tarragon

F

fenouil *m*	fennel
férule *f*	fennel florence (giant)
feuille *f* **de chêne**	oak leaf lettuce
feuille *f* **de laurier**	bay leaf
fèves - grosse	broad beans
figues *f*	figs
flageolets *m*	kidney beans; harricot beans
fond *m* **d'artichaut**	artichoke heart
fraises *f*	strawberries
fraises *f* **du bois**	wild strawberries
framboises *f*	raspberries
froment *m* (see also *blé*)	wheat

fruit *m*	fruit
fruit *m* **de bois**	wild fruit (berries)
fruit *m* **frais**	fresh fruit
fruit *m* **secs**	dried fruit

G

gingembre *m* **frais**	root / fresh ginger
girolle *f*	girolle mushroom
gousse *f* **d'ail**	clove of garlic
grappe *f* **de raisin**	bunch of grapes
grenade *f*	pomegranate
grenadine *f*	grenadine
griotte *f*	morello cherry
groseille blanche *f*	white currants
groseille *f* **a maquereau**	gooseberries
groseille *f* **verte**	gooseberries
groseille rouge *f*	red-currants

H

haricot *m* **d'espagne**	runner bean
haricot *m* **grimpant**	runner bean
haricots *m* **secs**	dried beans
haricots *m* **verts**	french green beans
haricots *m* **nain;**	kidney beans; harricot
harricot d'Espagne	beans

I

igname *f*   yam

K

kaki *m*   persimmon
kiwis *m*   kiwi fruit

L

lactaires *f*   milk cap mushrooms
laitue *f*   lettuce
laitue *f* **pommée**   cabbage lettuce
laitue *f* **romaine**   cos lettuce
lentille *f*   lentil
lentilles *f* **verte du puy**   puy lentils
luzerne *f*   alfalfa

M

mâche *f*   lamb's lettuce
maïs *m* **doux**   sweet corn
mandarine *f*   tangerine
mange-tout *m*   sugar peas
mangue *f*   mango
marjolaine *f*   marjoram
marron *f* (see also *châtaigne*)   chestnuts
melon *m*   melon

menthe *f*	mint
mirabelle *f*	type of plum
modeste *f*	chanterelle mushroom
moelle *f*	marrow
morille *f*	morel mushroom
mousserons *m*	fairy ring mushrooms
moutarde blanche et cresson alénois	mustard and cress
mûre *f*	blackberry
mûres *f*	mulberries
myrtille *f*	bilberry

N

navets *m*	turnips
navets *m* **de suède** (see also *rutabaga*)	swedes
nectarine *f* (see also *brugnon*)	nectarine
nèfle *f*	medlar
noisette *f*	hazelnuts
noix *f*	walnuts
noix *f* **de cajou**	cashew nuts
noix *f* **de coco**	coconut
noix *f* **de muscade**	nutmeg

O

oignons *m*	onions
olives *f*	olives
orge *f*	barley

origan *m*   wild marjoram
oseille *f*   sorrel

P

pamplemousse *m*   grapefruit
panais *m*   parsnip
paris *m* **bleu**   paris blue mushrooms
paris *m* **brun**   brown/chestnut mushroom
pieds *m* **bleu**   bluefoot or wood bluet mushrooms
pieds *m* **de mouton**   hedgehog mushrooms
pastéque *f*   water melon
patate *f* **douce**   sweet potato
pêches *f*   peaches
persil *m*   parsley
petit pois *m*   green peas
piment *m* **doux**   sweet pepper
piment *m* **rouge**   red chilli
piment *m* **vert**   green chille
pistache *f*   pistachio nut
plaintain *m*   plantain
pointe d'asperges   asparagus tips
poireau *m* (pl. *poireaux*)   leeks
poirée *f*   white beet
poires *f*   pears
pois *m* **cassés**   split peas

pois *m* **chiches**	chickpeas
pois *m* **chinois**	soya beans
citrouille poitron *m*	pumpkin
(see also *citrouille*)	
pomme á cuir	cooking apple
pomme *f*	apple (desert)
pomme *f* **sauvage**	crab apple
pommes *f* **de terre**	potato
pommes *f* **de terre au four**	baking potato
pommes *f* **de terre nouvelles**	new potato
pousse *f* **de soja**	bean sprouts
potiron *m*	pumpkin
prunelles *f*	sloes
prunes *f*	plums
pruneaux *f*	prunes
prunes *f* **de damas**	damsons

R

radis *m*	radish
raifort *m*	horseradish
raisins *m* **du table**	grapes (desert)
raisins *m* **secs**	raisins
raisins *m* **de corinthe**	currants
(see also *cassis*)	
reine-claude *f*	greengage
rhubarbe *f*	rhubarb
rocambole *f*	Spanish garlic

romarin *m* — rosemary
ronce-framboise *f* — loganberry
roquette *f* — rocket
rutabaga *m* — swede
(see also *navets de suède*)

S

salade *f* **verte** — green lettuce
salsifis *m* — salsify
sarriette *f* — savoury
sauge *f* — sage
scorsonère *f*; **salsifis noir** — scorzoneras
serpolet *m* — wild thyme

T

thym *m* — thyme
tomates *f* — tomatoes
topinambour *m* — jerusalen artichoke
trompettes *f* **de la morte** — trumpets of death mushrooms
truffe *f* — truffle

U

une asperges *f* — stick of asparagus

Poissons et Fruit de Mer

Fish and Shellfish

A

acarne *f* (see also *dorade*)	sea bream
aceline *f*	type of perch; see *perche*
actinie *f*	sea anenome
aiglefin *m*	haddock (fresh)
alevin *m*	fry
alose *f*	shad
alphée *f*	a crustacean
anchois *m*	anchovy
anguilles *f*	eels
anguille *f* **de mer**	conger eel
arraignée *f* **de mer**	spider crab

B

baleine *f*	whale
bar *m* (see also *loup de mer*)	sea bass
barbue *f* (see also *sandre*)	brill
barracuda *m*	barracuda
baudroie *f* (see also *lotte*)	monkfish
bigorneau *m*	winkle
bisque *f* **d'homard**	lobster soup

blanchailles *f*	whitebait
bonite *f*	bonito
boucards *m*	cockles
brème *f*	freshwater bream
brochet *m*	pike
bucardes *m*	see boucards
buccins *m*	whelks

C

cabillaud *m*	cod (fresh)
calmar *m*	calamari
carpe *f*	carp
carrelet *m*; (see also *plie*)	plaice
caviar *m*	caviar
chabot *m*	chubb
chair *f* **de crabe**	crabmeat
chien *m* **de mer**	dogfish
clovisse *f*	cockle
coalie *f*	coalfish
colin *m* (see also *merluche*)	hake
congre *m* **anguille** *f* **de mer**	conger eel
coque *f*	cockle
coquille *f* **Saint Jacques; escallops** *f*	scallops
côte *f* **de raie**	wing of skate
crabe *m*	crabmeat
craquelot *m* (see also *hareng bouffi*)	bloater
crevettes *f* **rose**	prawns

crevettes *f* **grise**   shrimps

D

darne *f*	slice/slab of salmon or cod
dorade *f*	sea bream
doré *m* **(jean)**	John Dory

E

écrevisse *f*	crayfish
encornet *m*	squid; calamar(i)
éperlan *m* (pl. *poissons des chenaux*)	smelts
escallops *f*	scallops
(see also *coquille f Saint Jacques*)	
espadon *m*	swordfish
esturgeon *m*	sturgeon

F

flet *m*	flounder
flétan *m*	halibut

G

gambas *f*	jumbo prawns
grondin *m* **gris**	gurnard/gurnet - grey
grondin *m* **rouge**	gurnard/gurnet - red
gujon *m*	gudgeon

H

haddock *m*	smoked haddock
hareng bouffi *m*	bloater
harengs *m*	herrings
harengs *m* **saurs**	red herrings
harenguets *m* (see also *sprat*)	sprats
homard *m*	lobster
huîtres *f*	oysters

J

jean doré *m*	John Dory

L

laitance *f*	soft roe
laitance *f* **du cabillaud**	cod's roe
laitance *f* **de morue**	
langoustine *f*	langoustine
langoustines *f*	scampi
lieu *m*	coley
lieu *m* **noir**	black pollack; saithe
lieu *m* **jaune**	yellow pollack
limande *f*	lemon sole
lingue *f* (see also *morue longue*)	ling
lotte *f* (see also *baudroie*)	monkfish
loup *m* **de mer** (see also *bar*)	sea bass

M

maquereau *m*	mackerel
merlan *m*	whiting
merlan *m* **jaune**	pollack
merluche *f* (see also *colin*)	hake
mérou *m*	grouper
morou *f* **longue** (see also *lingue*)	ling
morue *f* **seche**	cod - dry salted
moules *f*	mussels
mulet *m*	grey mullet

O

ombre *m*	grayling
orphie *f*	garfish
oursin *m*	sea urchin

P

palourdes *f* (see also *praires*)	clams
peau *f* **bleu**	shark
perche *f*	perch
pilchards *m*	pilchards
plie *f* (see also *carrelet*)	plaice
poisson-chat *m*	catfish
poulpe *m*	octopus
praires *f*	clams

R

raie *f*	skate
rascasse *f*	scorpion-fish; hog-fish
rouget *m*	red mullet
rousette *f*	rock salmon

S

sandre *f* (see also *barbue*)	brill
sardines *f*	sardines
saumon *m*	salmon
saumon *m* **fumée**	smoked salmon
seiche *f*	cuttlefish
sole *f*	sole
sole *f* **limande**	lemon sole
sprat *m* (see also *harenguets*)	sprats
St. Pierre *m*	John Dory

T

tacaud *m*	whiting / pout
tanche *f*	tench
thon *m*	tuna
torpille *f*	fish similar to skate
truite *f*	trout
truite *f* **saumonée**	salmon trout; sea trout
turbot *m*	turbot

Boulangerie

Dairy and Bakery

A

abaisse *f*	pastry rolled thin (base for cakes or tart)

B

babeurre *m*	buttermilk
baguette *f*	bread stick
beignets *m*	doughnuts
beurre *m*	butter
beurre *m* **demi sel**	butter slightly salted
beurre *m* **sans sel**	unsalted butter
bicarbonate *m* **de soude**	baking soda
biscotin *m*	crisp biscuit (served with ice cream)
biscotte *f*	dry toast
biscuit *m*	biscuit
biscuit *m* **à la cuillère**	sponge finger
biscuit *m* **au gingembre**	ginger biscuit
biscuit *m* **de savoie** (see also *génoise*)	sponge cake
biscuit *m* **fourrè au fromage**	cheese straws (fingers)
biscuit *m* **salé; biscuit** *m* **dur**	cracker

brioche *f*   soft sweet light dough
                                          baked like a cottage loaf
bûche *f* **de noël**   swiss roll

C

caillé *f*   curdled milk
caillebotte *f*   curds
caillette *f*   rennet
cake *m*   fruit cake
chapelures *f*   breadcrumbs
chausson *m* **au pommes**   puff pastry roll with
                                          apple filling
chou *m* **à la crème**   cream bun
crème *f*   cream
crème *f* **aigre**   soured cream
crème *f* **au lait**   custard
crème *f* **caillée (par échaudage)** clotted cream
crème *f* **chantilly**   whipped cream
crème *f* **fouettée**   whipped cream
crème *f* **fraîche**   double cream
crème *f* **fraîche liquide**   single cream
crème *f* **fleurette**   low fat cooking cream,
                                          (often used in place of
                                          crème fraîche)
crème *f* **légère**   light (thin) cream
crème *f* **semi epaisse**   half cream
croissant *m*   croissant
croûtons *m*   croutons

E

éclair *m*   éclair

F

farine *f*	flour
farine *f* complet	wholemeal flour
farine *f* d'avoine	oatmeal
farine *f* de blé; fleur de farine *f*	wheat flour
farine *f* de maïs	cornflour
farine *f* de siegle	rye flour
farine *f* lactée	malted milk flour
farine *f* pâtissière	pastry flour
farine *f* préparée à la levure chimique	self-raising flour
flûte *f*	long thin loaf of bread
fromage *m*	cheese
fromage *m* blanc	cream cheese - low fat
fromage *m* frais	soft cheese enriched with cream
fromage *m* à tartiner;	cream cheese
fromage *m* à la crème	cream cheese
fromage *m* de chèvre	goat's milk cheese
fromage *m* de vache	cow's milk cheese
fromage *m* fondu; fromage *f* industriel	processed cheese
fromage *m* maigre	low fat cheese

G

galette *f*	pancake
galette *f* **d'avoine**	oatcake
gateau *m* (pl. gateaux)	cake(s)
gaufrette *f*	wafer biscuit
génoise *f* (see also *biscuit de savoie*)	sponge cake
glace *f*	ice cream

L

lait *m*	cow's milk
lait *m* **de chèvre**	goat's milk
lait *m* **concentré**	evaporated milk
lait *m* **concentré sucré**	condensed milk
lait *m* **croissance**	milk for a growing child
lait *m* **demi-écrémé**	semi-skimmed milk
lait *m* **écrémé**	skimmed milk
lait *m* **en poudre**	powdered milk
lait *m* **homogénéisé(e)**	UHT milk
lait *m* **longue conservation**	long life milk
lait *m* **pour le bébé**	baby milk
lait *m* **entier**	full cream milk
levure *f*	yeast
levure *f* **chimique**	baking powder

M

macaron *m*	macaroon
margarene *f*	margarine
massepain *m*	marzipan
meringue *f*	meringue
miche *f* **de pain**	loaf of bread

O

œuf *f* (pl. *des œufs*)	egg(s)

P

pain *m*	bread
pain *m* **au bicarbonate de soude**	soda bread
pain *m* **au chocolat**	roll with chocolate filling
pain *m* **aux noix**	walnut bread
pain *m* **aux raisins**	roll with raisins
pain *m* **blanc**	white bread
pain *m* **complet**	wholemeal bread
pain *m* **complet; pain** *m* **bis**	brown bread
pain *m* **de campagne**	farmhouse bread
pain *m* **de froment**	wheat bread
pain *m* **de mie**	sandwich bread
pain *m* **de siegle**	rye bread
pain *m* **d'épice**	gingerbread cake
pains *m* **au lait**	scones

pain *m* **mollet**	soft bread ; bread roll
pain *m* **sans sel**	unsalted bread
pâte *f* (see also *pâtisserie*)	pastry
pâte *f* **brisée**	shortcrust pastry
pâte *f* **feuiletée**	puff pastry
pâte *f* **sablée**	sablée pastry
pâtisserie *f* **légère**	small cakes
pâtisserie *f* (see also *pâte*)	pastry
pavé *m*	slab of gingerbread
petit pain *m*	bread roll
petit pain *m* **en couronne**	bagel

S

sabayon *m*	zabaglione
sablé *m*	shortbread

T

tarte *f*	large tart
tarte *f* **au fromage blanc parfumée au citron**	cheesecake
tartelette *f*	small tart
tranche *f* **de pain**	slice of bread
tresse *f* **de pain**	plaited loaf

Y

yaourt *m*; **yoghourt** *m*	yoghurt

Vins et Spiriteux

Wines and Spirits

A

abricotine *f*　　　　　　　apricot brandy
armagnac *m*　　　　　　　armagnac

B

bière *f*　　　　　　　　　beer
brut　　　　　　　　　　dry; unsweetened
　　　　　　　　　　　　　(usually applied to
　　　　　　　　　　　　　champagne/white wine)

C

calvados *m*　　　　　　　apple brandy
cassis *m*, **crème de**　　　blackcurrant liqueur
champagne *f*　　　　　　champagne
chartreuse　　　　　　　brandy based liqueur,
　　　　　　　　　　　　　green or yellow
cidre *m*　　　　　　　　cider
crème *f* **de cacao**　　　　sweet cocoa-flavoured
　　　　　　　　　　　　　liqueur
crème *f* **de menthe**　　　pepermint-flavoured
　　　　　　　　　　　　　liqueur

cru *m*	locality of a vinyard

E

eau *f* **naturelle**	still water
eau *f* **gaseuse**	sparkling water
eau *f* **potable**	drinkable water
eau *f* **de vie**	fruit brandy
eau *f* **tonique** *m*	tonic water

F

fine champagne *f*	liqueur brandy

G

gin *m*	gin

M

médoc	wine (claret) growing area near Bordeaux

P

porto *m*	port

V

vin *m* **de bordeaux**	claret
vin *m* **de bourgoigne**	Burgundy (from Rhone valley region)

vin *m* **de premiè cuvée**   wine of the first growth
vin *m* **rosé**   rosé wine

X

xérès *m*   sherry

Épiceries

Grocery and Spices

A

abricot *m* **séché**	dried apricot
angélique	angelica
anis *m*	aniseed
aspic *m*	aspic jelly

B

barbeau *m* (see also *bleuet*)	cornflower
basilic *m*	basil
baies *f* **de genièvres**	juniper berries
bbq	American BBQ seasoning
bière *f*	beer
bisque *f*	shellfish soup
blé *m* **noir** (see also *sarasin*)	buckwheat
bleuet *m* (see also *barbeau*)	cornflower
bouillon *m* (liquide de cuisson or concentré)	stock (liquid or cubes)

C

cacao *m*	cocoa
café	coffee
café *m* **torréfié**	roasted coffee

cannelle *f*	cinnamon
câpres *f*	capers
câpres *f* **à l'eau salé**	capers in brine
cassonade *f*	soft brown sugar
céréals *f* **en flocons**	breakfast cereals
chapelure *f*	breadcrumbs (for frying)
chocolat *m* **à cuir**	cooking chocolate
chocolat *m* **fondant**	fondant chocolate
clous *m* **de girofle moulue**	cloves (ground)
clous *m* **de girofle entier**	cloves (whole)
coing *m*	quince
confiture(s) *f*	jam, preserve(s)
confiture *f* **d'agrumes**	citrus fruit jam
confiture *f* **d'orange**	marmalade (orange)
confiture *f* **de citron**	marmalade (lemon)
confiture *f* **de genièvre**	juniper-berry jam
cumin *m*	cumin

E

eau *f* **minérale naturelle**	mineral water - still
eau *f* **minérale naturelle gazeuse**	mineral water - sparkling
épices *f*	mixed spices
extrait *m* **de vanille**	vanilla essence

F

fécule *f* **de pommes de terre**	potato starch
fines herbes *f*	herb mixture of chopped chives, chervil, parsley, tarragon (dried)
fleur *f* **de muscade** (see also *macis*)	mace
fromage *f* **rapé**	grated cheese

G

gélatine *f*	gelatine
gingembre *m* **moloue**	ginger ground
glace *f*	ice cream
grains *m* **de café**	coffee beans
grains *m* **de carvi**	caraway seeds
graines *f* **de fenouil**	fennel seeds
grains *m* **de poivre**	pepper-corns
gras(se) *m*; **graisse** *f*	fat; lard
gras *m* **de porc**	pork fat
gras *m* **de canard**	duck fat
gras *m* **d'oie**	goose fat

H

haricots *m* **verts à la sauce tomate**	baked beans
huile *f* **d'olive**	olive oil
huile *f* **d'olive virgine**	olive oil first pressing

huile *f* **de tournesol**	sunflower oil
huile *f* **de vegetale**	vegetable oil
huile *f* **de colza**	rapeseed oil
huile *f* **de soja**	soya bean oil
huile *f* **d' arachide**	groundnut oil
huile *f* **de raisin**	grape seed oil
huile *f* **de truffe**	truffle oil
huile *f* **de noisette**	hazel nut oil

J

jus *m* **de fruit**	fruit juice
jus *m* **d'orange**	orange juice
jus *m* **de tomates**	tomato juice

L

langues *f* **d'oiseau**	birds eye chillies
levure *f* **de boulangerie**	baker's yeast
levure *f* **chimique**	baking powder

M

macis *m* (see also *fleur de muscade*)	mace
macaroni *m*	macaroni
marmelade *f*	compote (puree) of fruit
massepain *m*	marzipan
marrons *m* **glacé**	chestnuts in syrup
miel *m*	honey

mignonette *f*	coarse ground white pepper
moutarde *f*	mustard
moutarde *f* **de dijon**	Dijon mustard

N

noix *f* **de muscade**	nutmeg
(des) nouilles *f*	noodles, spaghetti, etc.
(see also *pâtes alimentaires*)	

O

olives *f* **dénoyautée**	stoned olives
olives *f* **farci**	stuffed olives
orge *f* **perlé**	pearl barley
origan *m*	oregano

P

paprika *m*	paprika
parmesan *m*	parmesan
pâtes *f* **alimentaires**	noodles, spaghetti, etc.
pétoncle *m*	pastry case, scallop-shaped
piment *m* **de la Jamaïque**	allspice
pois *m* **chiche**	chick-peas
poivre *m*	pepper
poivre *m* **blanc**	white pepper

poivre *m* **noir** black pepper
poivre *m* **de cayenne** cayenne pepper

R

rillettes *f* potted meat, cooked
and shredded (pork,
duck, game, chicken)

S

saffran *m* saffron
salicorne *f* grasswort
sarrasin *m* (see also *blé noir*) buckwheat
sauce *f* **au raifort** horseradish sauce
sauce *f* **piquante (en bouteille)** tomato ketchup
à base de tomates
sauce *f* **rouille** fish soup sauce
sauce *f* **soja** soy sauce
sel *m* salt
sel *m* **blanc** table salt
sel *m* **gros** coarse salt
sel *m* **fin** fine salt
sel *m* **de mer** sea salt
sel *m* **culinaire** cooking salt
sel *m* **de céleri** celery salt
semoule *f* semolina
soupe *f* **de poisson** fish soup

sucre *m*	sugar
sucre *m* **semoule**	caster sugar
sucre *m* **roux**	brown sugar

V

vanille *f*	vanilla
vermicelles *f*	vermicelli
vinaigre *m*	vinegar
vinaigre *m* **du cidre**	cider vinegar
vinaigre *m* **de noisette**	hazelnut vinegrette
vinaigre *m* **de malt**	malt vinegar
vinaigre *m* **de vin**	wine vinegar

Helpful Information

Liquid measures

a litre	un litre *m*
a carafe e.g. of wine	un quart e.g. de vin (25cl or 50cl)

Solid measures

piece of (e.g. cheese, meat)	un morceau
pinch (e.g. of salt)	pincée *f* (de sel)
spoonful	cuillerée *f*
desertspoonful	cuillerée *f* à dessert
tablespoonful	cuillerée *f* à bouche
teaspoon measure	petite cullère *f*
sprinkle (e.g. of salt, sugar)	saupoudrer (de sel; du sucre)
sprinkle (of herbs)	parsemer (de . . .)

Weights

a kilogramme (1,000g = 2.2 lbs)	un kilo *m*
half a kilo (500g = 1.1 lbs)	un demi kilo *m*
a pound (approx half a kilo)	une livre *f*

Converting weights

ounces > grams	-	multiply ounces by 28.3495
grams > ounces	-	divide grams by 28.3495
pounds > kilos	-	multiply pounds by 0.4536
kilos > pounds	-	divide kilograms by 0.4536

Temperatures

Gas mark	Fahrenheit	Centigrade
0.5	250	121
1	275	135
2	300	149
3	325	163
4	350	177
5	375	190
6	400	204
7	425	218
8	450	232
9	475	246

Useful adjectives

General

hard (tough)	dur
soft	mollet
dry	sec *m;* sèche *f*
thick	épais *m;* épaisse *f*
thicker	plus épais (épaisse)
thin	mince
thinner	plus mince
more (than that)	plus (que ça . . .)
less (than that)	moins (que ça . . .)

Meat & Fish

uncooked / raw	cru
very underdone, almost raw	bleu
underdone	pas assez cuit; pas trop cuit; saignant
well cooked (well done)	bien cuit
boned (meat)	désossé
fat removed	dégraissé
hung meat or game	mortifié(e);
well hung	bien mortifié(e)
salted / pickled	salé(e)

Fruit & Vegetables

unripe	pas mûr
ripe	mûr

Cheese

ripe	fromage *m* bien fait
mild	fromage *m* doux
hard	fromage *m* dur

Containers, hardware and cooking aids

bag	sac *m*
plastic bag	sac *m* plastique
bottle	bouteille *f*
half bottle	demi-bouteille *f*
box	boîte *f*
box of matches	boîte *f* d'allumettes
charcoal	charbon *m* de bois
tin/can	boïte *m* (metalique)
tin opener	ouvre-boïte *m*
tinned food	conserves *f* alimentaires en boite
cork	bouchon *m*
corkscrew	tire bouchon *m*
firelighter	allume-feu *m*
greaseproof paper	papier *m* parcheminé

Check-out and paying

basket	panier *m*
cashier	caissier *m* cassière *f*
change (cash)	monnaie *f*
check-out	caisse *f*
queue	queue *m*
money	argent *m*
receipt	reçu *m*
refund	remboursement *m*
trolley	chariot *m*

Cooking verbs

to roast	rôtir
to boil	bouiller
to fry	(faire) frire
to cook in a frying pan	poêler

Cleaning & hygiene

air freshener	désodorisant *m*
detergent	produit *m* de nettoyage
fly spray	bombe *f* insecticide
hair shampoo	shampooing *m*
household bleach	eau *f* de javel
soap	savon *m*
toilet paper	papier *m* toilette
washing powder	lessive *f* en poudre
washing-up liquid	liquide *m* en vaisselles

First aid

thermometer	thermomètre *m*
cotton wool	ouate *f*
bandage	sparadrap *m*
sticking plaster	pansement *m* adhésif
a burn	une brûlure *f*
sunburn	coup *m* de soleil
wound (cut)	coupure *f*
broken leg, arm	jambe cassée, bras *m* cassé
doctor	médecin *m*, docteur *m*
dentist	dentiste *m/f*
the hospital	l'hôpital *m*
chemist's shop	pharmacie *f*
hot water bottle	bouillotte *f*
veterinary surgery	vétérinaire *f*

Common phrases

I am looking for	je, cherche .....
Where do I find... please	s'il vous plaît, ou je trouve......
Please can I make an appointment with.....	s'il vous plaît, puis je fait un rendezvous avec.....

Alphabet	Phonetic pronunciation
A	ah (a short sharp syllable - like 'uh')
B	beh
C	ceh (not drawn out like 'say')
D	deh
E	euh (extend your lips forward then say 'ee')
F	eff
G	jeh (the 'j' is softer than in English)
H	ash
I	ee
J	jee (the 'j' is softer than in English)
K	kah (a short sharp syllable)
L	ell
M	emm
N	enn
O	ohh
P	peh
Q	ku
R	aihr
S	ess
T	tay
U	eu
V	veh (as in very)
W	doobleveh
X	eeks
Y	eegrek
Z	zed

Numerals

1	one *m*	urn (say 'urn' but don't pronounce the 'n') In front of a consonant keep the word separate from the following word e.g. a small car - 'urn petee orto' but an egg - 'ur n'erf'
	one *f*	oon (in front of a female gender noun e.g. a girl - 'oon famm')
2-10	two	duh
	three	trwoi
	four	kattre
	five	sank
	six	see (before a consonant) or cease (before a vowel or 'h') e.g. six o'clock - 'cease heures' or six kilos - 'see kilos'
	seven	sett
	eight	wheat
	nine	nurf
	ten	dee (before a consonant) or deece (before a vowel or 'h') e.g. ten o'clock - 'deece heures' or ten minutes - 'dee minootes'

11-19	eleven	onze
	twelve	dooze
	thirteen	trays
	fourteen	kattorze
	fifteen	kanze
	sixteen	seze
	seventeen	deece-set
	eighteen	deece-wheat
	nineteen	deece-nurf
20	twenty	van ('van' but don't pronounce the 'n')
	twenty-one	vantayurn (see 'one' above)
	twenty-two	van duh
	twenty-three	van trwoi
	twenty-four	van kattre
	twenty-five	van sank
	twenty-six	van cease
	twenty-seven	van sett
	twenty-eight	vant wheat
	twenty-nine	van nurf
30	thirty	traunt
	thirty-one	trauntayurn
	thirty-two	traunt duh
40	forty	karraunt
	forty-one	karrauntayurn
	forty-two	karraunt duh

50	fifty	sankaunt
	fifty-one	sankauntayurn
	fifty-two	sankaunt duh
60	sixty	swassaunt
	sixty-one	swassauntayurn
	sixty-two	swassaunt duh
70	seventy	swassaunt deece
	seventy-one	swassauntay onze
	seventy-two	swassaunt dooze
	seventy-three	swassaunt trays
	seventy-four	swassaunt kattorze
	seventy-five	swassant kanze
	seventy-six	swassant seze
	seventy-seven	swassant deece sett
	seventy-eight	swassant deece wheat
	seventy-nine	swassant deece nurf
80	eighty	kattre van
	eighty-one	kattre vantayurn
	eighty-two	kattrevan duh
90	ninety	kattrevan deece
	ninety-one	kattrevantay onze
	ninety-two	kattrevan dooze
100	one hundred	song (rhymes with 'gone' but don't pronounce the 'g')

	two hundred	duh song
	three hundred	trwoi son
	four hundred	kattre song
	five hundred	sank song
	six hundred	seece song
	seven hundred	sett song
	eight hundred	wheat song
	nine hundred	nurf song
1000	one thousand	meal
	two thousand	duh meal

Harriman House

Harriman House specialises in publishing books about money, investment and property abroad. This dictionary is the first in a series for buyers of French property, and is a natural complement to our flagship product – **The French Property Buyer's Handbook**, details of which are provided overleaf.

If you would like a free copy of Harriman's latest catalogue, please contact us by one of the following methods:

phone:	01730 233870
email:	bookshop@harriman-house.com
post:	Harriman House
	43 Chapel Street
	Petersfield
	GU32 3DY
online:	www.harriman-house.com

For a broader range of books on French property, we recommend BooksOnFrance.com:

www.booksonfrance.com

which carries hundreds of books covering property purchase, building, taxation and all other aspects of owning a property in France.

The French Property Buyer's Handbook

Everything you need to know about buying a house and moving to France

by Natalie Avella

- choosing the right area
- the different property styles
- looking for the right property
- dealing with property agents
- building your own house
- arranging finance for the purchase
- negotiating the property transaction
- moving into your new house
- getting all the paperwork right
- opening bank accounts and tax
- health and the French social security system
- running a gîte business
- finding a job or starting a business in France

Plus hundreds of tips and practical advice on all those small matters that are key to making your purchase in France a success.

All this is explained in straightforward language, supported by a wealth of tables, contact details for further information, and case studies of people who have bought in France.

Is this book for you?

The book is for anyone looking to buy a property in France to use as a holiday home, to work from, or to start a new life abroad.

It can be used as an active reference guide when 'on the ground' in France, getting up early for that 8am appointment with an *immobilier*, but can also be used by people just thinking about moving to France who are not quite ready to make the move yet. The book highlights all the issues that you need to consider.

Whether you're looking to buy an old farm, a new house, an apartment, share a property or set up a gîte complex, this book covers you all the way.

Publisher: Harriman House
ISBN: 1897597371
Format: Paperback
Date: July 2004
Pages: 250
Illustrations: 30 line drawings
Maps: 40
Price: £12.99

Order hotline
01730 233870